What Puppies Teach Us

WILLOW CREEK PRESS

Minocqua, Wisconsin

Published by Willow Creek Press
P.O. Box 147
Minocqua, Wisconsin 54548
www.willowcreekpress.com

Editor: Andrea Donner

Library of Congress Cataloging-in-Publication Data

Dromgoole, Glenn.
   What puppies teach us : life's lessons learned from our little friends / Glenn Dromgoole.
      p. cm.
Summary: Photographs of puppies and simple text reminding the reader of such lessons as "Friendship means caring and sharing," "Be careful in traffic," and "Be willing to learn new things."
   ISBN 1-57223-684-1 (hardcover : alk. paper)
1. Puppies--Miscellanea--Juvenile literature. 2. Puppies--Pictorial works--Juvenile literature. [1. Dogs--Habits and behavior. 2. Animals--Infancy. 3. Behavior. 4. Conduct of life.] I. Title.
   SF426.5.D77 2003
   636.7'07--dc21
                                    2003000114

Printed in Canada

© Norvia Behling

Smile — someone
is sure to smile back.

It's fun to play with **friends**...

...but make up your **own** games if nobody is around to play with you.

Falling down **hurts,**
but **not** for long.

Be **curious** about the world around you.
There's a lot to **learn**!

Help others whenever you can.

Some **friends** don't look anything like you.

Keep on trying ...

... until you get it **right**.

If you're **patient,**
you'll get what you're after.

No matter
what you do,
somebody
loves you
just because
you're **you!**

You're never too small to make your own music.

Be **careful** around strangers.

It's fun to **run**, and **jump**, and **play**…

...but remember to
rest sometimes, too.

Be **thankful** when you get a special treat.

Say you're **sorry**
  if you hurt someone.

Teasing is never nice.

Cheer up
others
when
they're
sad.

Listen when someone is talking to you.

Don't be **afraid** to try new things.

Once in a while,
tell somebody you **love** them.

Laugh
out loud if
something
is **funny**.

Pick up your **toys** when you are finished playing.

Include **everybody** when
you play games.

Be **kind**
to those
littler
than you.

Like it or not,
sometimes you have to take a bath.

It isn't easy, but you need
to learn how to **share**.

Sometimes it feels good to be
quiet and **still**.

Be happy about going to bed
where you can sleep and dream.